DERRY - LONDONDERRY: GATEWAY TO A NEW WORLD

The story of emigration from the Foyle by sail and steam

Brian Mitchell

CLEARFIELD

Originally published:
Londonderry, Northern Ireland
2014

Reprinted for Clearfield Company by
Genealogical Publishing Company
Baltimore, Maryland
2014

ISBN 978-0-8063-5691-4

Front cover illustration:
"Londonderry" from an original sketch by John Nixon, circa 1790

Back cover illustration:
Anchor Line advertising poster depicting Caledonia

About the Author

Brian Mitchell has been researching local, family, and emigration history in Derry since 1982. He supervised the construction of a database containing one million records (dating from 1642 to 1922), extracted from the major civil and church registers of County Derry, which is now accessible at www.derry.rootsireland.ie.

Previous local history publications include:

On the Banks of the Foyle: Historic Photographs of Victorian and Edwardian Derry
Derry: A City Invincible
The Making of Derry: An Economic History
The Surnames of Derry
Historic Eglinton - A Thriving Ornament

DERRY~ LONDONDERRY: GATEWAY TO A NEW WORLD
The story of emigration from the Foyle by sail and steam
by Brian Mitchell

From the late 1600s, in the age of the sailing ships, to the onset of the Second World War in 1939, when the last transatlantic steamer sailed from the port, Derry~Londonderry was one of the principal emigration ports in Ireland.

17th Century Emigrants

Derry port possessed an ideal situation. She stood at the head of a virtually land-locked Lough Foyle, 24 miles long and only 2 miles wide at its head. The Lough was sheltered from the prevailing westerly winds by the Inishowen peninsula, thus making it, in the age of sail, a harbour of refuge, accessible and safe in all weathers. Owing to her westerly situation Derry was seen as being halfway between London and the American colonies; a Derry ship "is no sooner out of the river, but she is immediately in the open sea and has but one course."

Derry was, therefore, well placed to benefit from the emigration of Ulster people to North America. From about 1680 a trickle of north Irish emigrants arrived in the American colonies. This movement was mainly confined to the Laggan (County Donegal) and Foyle valleys (Counties Derry and Tyrone).

The Reverend Francis Makemie (1658-1708) of Ramelton, County Donegal, ordained in 1682 by the Presbytery of Laggan, travelled from the port of Londonderry to the American colonies as a minister/missionary. In 1683, Makemie established four Presbyterian congregations, including Rehoboth, Maryland. Since Makemie was under the Presbytery of Laggan's direction, these churches often are claimed to be the first Presbyterian churches in America. In 1706, Makemie helped bring together Presbyterian ministers and elders to establish the Presbytery of Philadelphia. This was the official birth of American Presbyterianism.

Robert Bruce Pollock emigrated from Derry with his family, consisting of his wife Magdalen and two children, to Somerset County in Maryland between 1672 and 1680. Robert Bruce Pollock, born in Scotland, had settled in the Lifford area of east Donegal during the 17th century Plantation of Ulster. Robert was the great-great-great-grandfather of James Knox Polk, the 11th President of the USA from 1845-1849. Born 2 November 1795, near Charlotte in North Carolina, James Knox Polk settled with his family, after a 500-mile journey, at Duck River, in 1806, close to the present-day town of Columbia in Tennessee, USA.

18th Century Emigration and the Ulster-Scots

Between 1718 and the beginning of the War of American Independence in 1776, 250,000 Ulster-Scots – often referred to as Scotch-Irish or Scots-Irish in USA (i.e. descendants of 17th century Scottish Presbyterian settlers in the nine counties of the Province of Ulster: Antrim, Armagh, Down, Fermanagh, Londonderry and Tyrone in Northern Ireland and Cavan, Donegal and Monaghan in the Republic of Ireland) – emigrated from Ireland through the ports of Belfast, Londonderry, Newry, Larne and Portrush for the British Colonies in North America.

The first step in what was to become a large-scale exodus of Ulster-Scots occurred in 1718 when one thousand northern Irish people disembarked at Boston from ten vessels which had departed from Londonderry and Coleraine. The bulk of these early emigrants arriving in Boston in 1718 came from the Foyle (Counties Derry, Donegal and Tyrone) and Bann valleys (Counties Derry and Antrim). James MacGregor, son of Captain MacGregor of Magilligan and minister of Aghadowey Presbyterian Church, accompanied some of his congregation to Boston and they established, in 1719, the settlement of Londonderry, New Hampshire.

Later Ulster-Scot emigrants who departed through Derry founded the settlements of Londonderry, Nova Scotia (Canada) in 1770 and Londonderry, New Brunswick (Canada) in 1818.

Conditions on board 18th century emigrant ships were harsh. Disease thrived on overcrowded ships, with all emigrants accommodated, in communal berths, in the space between decks – the height between decks seldom exceeded 5 feet 6 inches; four feet six inches was common. Port holes to provide ventilation and light were non-existent. Further hazards included storms, shipwreck and even capture by French and Spanish privateers. By the 1770s the voyage across the Atlantic, on average, took 7 weeks with the fastest being 27 days by *Jupiter* to Philadelphia from Derry in 1772 and the slowest being 17 weeks by *General Wolfe* also to Philadelphia from Derry in the same year.

Faithful Steward

General Robert E Lee who led the Confederate forces during the American Civil War (1861-1865) shared a family connection with James Lee who left Londonderry, destined for Philadelphia, on the *Faithful Steward* in July 1785. James Lee was accompanied by his parents, three brothers, two sisters, a brother's wife, three uncles, three aunts, and thirty-three cousins; in all, 48 of the Lee family connection sailed on board the *Faithful Steward*.

The *Faithful Steward*, with 249 passengers and 13 crew, was shipwrecked within 100 yards of the Delaware coast on 1 September 1785. There were only 68 survivors – 13 crew, 10 cabin passengers and 45 steerage passengers. Only seven women survived. All of the Lee connection, except James Lee and a brother's wife and four cousins, were drowned.

Philadelphia

The emigration trade established Derry as one of the chief Irish ports for transatlantic trade in the 18th century. In 1771 the American colonies took more linen cloth and provisions from Derry than Britain did, and thirty percent of Ulster-Scots, around 75,000 people, emigrated through Derry port to North America prior to 1776 and the American Declaration of Independence.

Links between the cities of Londonderry and Philadelphia were established, through trade, in the 18th century. Flaxseed, the raw material of the linen industry, was shipped to Derry from Philadelphia in the early spring, and on the return voyage linen and emigrants were destined for Philadelphia.

It is clear that strong trade links, reinforced by family connections in the mercantile community, developed in the 18th century between the ports of Londonderry and Philadelphia.

Captain Conolly McCausland of Streeve Hill (near Limavady) was assisting mass emigration from the Roe Valley, County Derry as commander of ships, *Walworth*, *Jane* and *Faithful Steward* during the American Revolutionary period, 1768-1785. Conolly and his brother Abraham McCausland, merchant of Londonderry, were engaged in transatlantic trade together with their cousins Robert McCausland of Coleraine and John Stirling of Walworth (near Ballykelly).

Conolly McCausland captained the ship *Walworth* on a dozen or more voyages across the Atlantic between 1768 and 1773. The *Walworth* was a joint venture with Strabane-born Thomas Barclay of Philadelphia. Barclay followed his uncle Samuel Carsan, also a Strabane emigrant, to Philadelphia, then the largest port in America. Carsan, joint owner of over 20 ships, built up the Philadelphia mercantile firm of Carsan and Davey. In the 1760s with Thomas Barclay's arrival, a new partnership emerged: Carsan, Barclay and Mitchell. The third principal was William Mitchell, the son of James Mitchell of Londonderry.

The Frontier

The Ulster-Scots tended to enter America through Philadelphia and then head for the frontier. Of 128 vessels advertised to sail from Derry between 1750 and 1775, 99 (77%) sailed for Philadelphia with 10 each destined for Charleston (in South Carolina) and Nova Scotia (Canada).

From Philadelphia the Ulster-Scots then poured across the Susquehanna into the Cumberland Valley. From the 1740s they moved southwards through the Great Valley, east of the Appalachian Mountains, across the Potomac and into the Shenandoah Valley (also known as the Valley of Virginia) between the Blue Ridge and Appalachian ranges. From there they continued south into the Piedmont of North and South Carolina. By the Revolutionary War, in 1776, about 90% of Ulster settlers had made their homes in Pennsylvania, the Valley of Virginia and the Carolinas; and they dominated a one thousand mile frontier along the spine of Appalachia from Pennsylvania to South Carolina.

It was said of the early settlers in Pennsylvania that the Quakers were better traders, the Germans better farmers and the Ulster-Scots were best at coping with frontier conditions. In the words of one Colonial administrator the Ulster-Scots were "troublesome settlers to the Government and hard neighbours to the Indians."

With the War of American Independence over the Ulster-Scots then spearheaded the first thrusts across the Appalachian range, through the Cumberland Gap, into Kentucky and Tennessee. By 1792, 100,000 people had moved into the frontier lands through the Cumberland Gap along the Wilderness Road.

James Buchanan of Ramelton, County Donegal departed from Londonderry for Philadelphia on the ship *Providence* on 4 June 1783. James established a trading post at Cove Gap, Pennsylvania in the Allegheny Mountains, married Elizabeth Spear, and, on 23 April 1791, their son, James Buchanan, who was to become the 15th President of the USA from 1857 to 1861, was born.

Stephen Collins Foster

Stephen Collins Foster, born 4 July 1826 at Pittsburgh, has been described as the 'Father of American music' and 'one of the iconic figures in the Ulster-Scots Diaspora.' Stephen Foster's great-grandfather, Alexander Foster, emigrated from Londonderry, as a 15-year-old boy, in 1725 and settled at Lancaster, Pennsylvania.

Inducted into the Nashville Songwriters Hall of Fame in 2010, Stephen Collins Foster's songs – such as Oh! Susanna, Camptown Races, Hard Times Come Again No More, My Old Kentucky Home, Jeanie with the Light Brown Hair and Beautiful Dreamer – remain popular over 150 years after their composition.

19th Century Emigration in the Age of Sail

There is still a tendency to see the Famine of 1846 to 1851, when over a million people left Ireland for North America, as the cause of the Irish Diaspora. In reality heavy emigration from Ireland began well before the Famine and continued well after it. With the end of the Napoleonic Wars in 1815 many small farmers, agricultural labourers and rural tradesmen in Ireland saw emigration as the only solution to their declining economic prospects. Emigration thus acted as a "safety valve," enabling young men and women with little economic prospects to escape Ireland.

Derry's importance as an emigration port continued to grow in the 19th century; it was a profitable trade. Merchants in Derry soon became ship-owners as opposed to agents for American and British companies. An outward cargo of emigrants, a homeward cargo of timber or grain, together with two voyages per year, one in spring and one in the autumn, ensured a sizeable profit. By 1833 seven merchants in the city – Daniel Baird, James Corscaden, John Kelso, William McCorkell, James McCrea, John Munn and Joseph Young – owned fifteen vessels, all engaged in the North American emigrant trade.

Saint John (New Brunswick) and Quebec in Canada, and New York and Philadelphia in the United States were the destination ports of emigrants departing from Derry in the first half of the 19th century. Of 38 emigrant ships advertised to sail from Derry in 1836: 12 were destined for Saint John (New Brunswick), 12 for Philadelphia, 7 for Quebec and 6 for New York.

In this period the merchant community of Derry established close trading links with their counterparts in Liverpool (England), Glasgow (Scotland), Philadelphia (USA) and the province of New Brunswick, Canada. An examination of shipping registers for the period 1834 to 1850, recorded in Derry's Custom House, details 54 ships, over 100 tons in size, belonging to the merchant community of Derry. Twenty-eight of these ships were built in Canada (16 of them in the Province of New Brunswick) and 19 in Scotland

Sickness and Shipwreck

Sickness and shipwreck were two hazards faced by emigrants on board sailing ships departing Derry in this period.

The *John Stamp* arrived in Philadelphia from Derry in June 1832 and Philip Duffy, a railway contractor, hired 57 men from this ship to construct 'mile 59', or 'Duffy's Cut' through the

Malvern Valley, of the 80 mile stretch of railway between Philadelphia and Columbia. All these men died, probably from cholera, in 'Dead Horse Hollow,' Chester County, Pennsylvania in the summer of 1832.

Europe was in the grips of a cholera epidemic and it spread to North America. The *Londonderry Sentinel* of Saturday 18 August 1832 recorded the deaths of 361 people in Quebec, from cholera, with "passengers susceptible to the disease after a long sea voyage." It further reported that "the cholera is very bad in New York – it is said that 100,000 inhabitants had fled the city."

The *Exmouth* departed Derry on 25 April 1847 for Quebec with 208 emigrants and it was wrecked off Islay (Scotland) with only three survivors (who were crew members). Passengers on the *Exmouth* were named in the *Londonderry Journal* of 12 May 1847 and a memorial was erected to them in Islay in 2000.

The death rate at sea increased twelve-fold during the famine years (1846-1851). Ship fever left sixty of the *Superior's* 360 passengers dead before they arrived at Quebec in 1847. On her last voyage to Philadelphia in 1853 the *Envoy* was forced back by heavy weather to Lough Foyle where sixty-three of her passengers drowned when abandoning her.

J & J Cooke

By the 1850s, two local companies, J & J Cooke and William McCorkell & Co., dominated transatlantic trade and, in the process, built up sizeable shipping fleets.

In 1837 John Cooke and his brother Joseph began a partnership that lasted until John Cooke's death on 25 February 1895. Between 1847 and 1867 J & J Cooke carried 22,199 passengers to North America. In this period the firm bought nine ships specifically for the emigration trade. At the height of the Famine in 1847, of 12,385 emigrants leaving from Derry, 5,104 or 41% were carried by J & J Cooke in 20 ships; 8 of these ships were destined for Philadelphia, 7 for Saint John, New Brunswick and 5 for Quebec.

Prior to the 1860s, and the establishment of a railway network in Ireland, the port of Derry served as the emigration port for Counties Derry, Donegal and Tyrone. An examination of the order book of J & J Cooke, for 1850, confirms that 88% of passengers carried on their ships came from these three counties; with 40% from Donegal, 26% from Tyrone and 22% from Derry.

The Inishowen peninsula, County Donegal was home to many emigrants through the port of Derry. For example, when the *Marchioness of Clydesdale*, contracted by J & J Cooke, sailed out of Derry for Saint John, New Brunswick, at the height of the Famine in 1847, she was carrying 168 emigrants from Inishowen, including 87 people from Carndonagh, 23 from Clonmany, 15 from Malin and 11 from Culdaff.

William McCorkell & Co.

William McCorkell, born in 1728, was the founder of the Londonderry shipping line, William McCorkell & Co., in 1778. Initially the company acted as agents for American-owned ships in the passenger trade from Londonderry to North America. In 1815, they bought their first ship, the *Marcus Hill*, for the passenger trade. From 1815 until 1897 when their last vessel, the *Hiawatha*, was sold the McCorkell Line owned 26 ships.

NOW IN PORT.
NOTICE TO PASSENGERS.

Those Persons who have taken their Passages by the First Class Coppered Ship

SUPERIOR,
CAPTAIN MASON,
FOR QUEBEC,

Are required to be in Derry on TUESDAY, the 13th of JULY, pay the remainder of their Passage Money, and go on Board, as the Vessel will sail first fair wind after that date. A few more Passengers will be taken, on moderate terms, if immediate application is made to

Mr. DAVID MITCHELL, *Dungiven,* or the Owners,

J. & J. COOKE.

Derry, June 28, 1847.

The *Superior*, 751 tons, was built in Prince Edward Island, Canada and purchased, in 1845, by John and Joseph Cooke, timber and emigration merchants, Londonderry. The death rate at sea during the famine years (1846 to 1851) increased twelve-fold; ship fever left sixty of the *Superior's* 360 passengers dead before they arrived at Quebec in 1847.

The Catchment Area of Derry Port for the Emigrant Trade to North America in 1850

Ballymoney

Coleraine
Limavady
Ballykelly
Dungiven
Draperstown
Claudy
DERRY
Donemana
Gortin
Culdaff
Carndonagh
Moville
Ture
Muff
Strabane
Newtownstewart
Castlederg
Malin
Burt
Lifford
Ardstraw
Drumquin
Omagh
Beragh
Six Mile Cross
Fintona
Clonmany
Carrigart
Raphoe
Convoy
Castlefin
Ramelton
Killeter
Kesh
Dunfanaghy
Letterkenny
Cross
Donegal
Ederny
Enniskillen
Ballyshannon

SCALE

0   15
  MILES

KEY

. . . .   County Boundary

•   Districts from which 10 or more people emigrated through
    the port of Derry on J & J Cooke ships in 1850.

—   The hinterland of Derry Port for the Emigrant Trade.

9

In the 1860s the McCorkell Line demonstrated that first-class sailing ships could compete with steam on the North American passenger run. They had five ships plying between Derry and the US cities of New York and Philadelphia: the *Mohongo*, *Minnehaha*, *Stadacona*, *Village Belle* and *Lady Emily Peel*. *Minnehaha*, the McCorkell flagship, which was known in New York as "the green yacht from Derry," maintained a passenger service of two voyages per year to New York throughout the American Civil War (1861-1865).

By the 1870s sailing ships could no longer compete with the speed, comfort and reliability of the transatlantic passenger steamers. In 1873 the *Minnehaha* made the last passenger voyage by a Derry-owned ship to New York. The *Minnehaha* then became, for the next fourteen years, a Baltimore grain carrier. Indeed, from 1873 to 1889 the McCorkell Line bought seven ships, principally for the Baltimore grain trade and, by 1881, they had a fleet of eight ships constantly employed in the Baltimore grain run.

Pre-paid Passage Certificates

From its earliest days Irish migration has been a family affair. The Irish either moved with kin or moved to join kin. By the nineteenth century the emigrant trade in Derry depended to a large extent on people in North America paying the fare to bring out family and friends.

The Passenger Book of J & J Cooke records the names and addresses of 22,199 emigrants carried on their ships from Derry to North America between 1847 and 1867, many of whom held pre-paid passage certificates that had been purchased in the office of J & J Cooke's agent in Philadelphia, Andrew J. Catherwood.

The order book of Robert Taylor and Co. of Philadelphia, dating from November 1863 to April 1871, records the names and addresses of 5,184 Irish emigrants who were 'engaged' in Philadelphia, i.e. in receipt of pre-paid passage, to sail from Derry on ships of the McCorkell Line.

Liverpool

From the 1830s to the 1860s the port of Liverpool emerged as the preferred port of embarkation for Irish emigrants destined for North America. By the Famine the Liverpool-New York route was the main artery of Irish emigration. New York received about 67% of the total number of Irish who emigrated to the US between 1848 and 1851. In the same period nearly 74% of Irish emigrants departed from Liverpool with Irish ports carrying only 20% of Famine emigrants.

The introduction of regular steamboat services in the 1820s to Liverpool and Glasgow from Derry facilitated the transport of intending emigrants from Derry to North America and Australia, via Liverpool and Glasgow. By 1836 the Londonderry and Glasgow Steamboat Company had three boats operating on the Glasgow route and the North West of Ireland Union Steam Company ran two boats on the Liverpool route.

Cross-Channel Emigration and the Scotch Boat

Steamer connections, established from the 1820s, between Irish ports and the ports of Liverpool and Glasgow transported large numbers of Irish emigrants to the cities of a rapidly growing industrial Britain.

List of Passengers who departed Londonderry in Spring 1853 for Philadelphia on J & J Cooke ship *Superior*

No.	Date	NAME	RESIDENCE	Age	Passage
1706	March 24	James Greer	Ramelton	13	On Mr Catherwood's order
1705	March 24	Susan Greer	Ramelton	13	On Mr Catherwood's order
1703	March 24	Jane Russell	Ramelton		On Mr Catherwood's order
1692	March 24	Hugh Sweeny	Creeslough		On Mr Catherwood's order
1711	March 24	Mary Arnott	Stranorlar		On Mr Catherwood's order
1672	March 24	Thomas McGarvey	Fannett		On Mr Catherwood's order
1685	March 24	Margaret Moffatt	Fannett		On Mr Catherwood's order
1697	March 24	Cecilia Dougherty	Clonmany		On Mr Catherwood's order
	March 24	Mary Deeny	Carn		On Mr Catherwood's order
	March 24	Joseph Deeny	Carn	12	On Mr Catherwood's order
	March 24	Hugh Deeny	Carn	9	On Mr Catherwood's order
	March 24	John Deeny	Carn	7	On Mr Catherwood's order
1701	March 24	Thos Herritt	Cross		On Mr Catherwood's order
1702	March 24	Jack Mulloy	Ballygorman		On Mr Catherwood's order
1695	March 24	Sarah Dougherty	Malin		On Mr Catherwood's order
1696	March 24	Bridget Dougherty	Malin	7	On Mr Catherwood's order
1714	March 24	John Dougherty	Malin		On Mr Catherwood's order
1713	March 24	Nancy Gallagher	L.Derry		On Mr Catherwood's order
1719	March 24	Catharine Stewart	L.Derry		On Mr Catherwood's order
	March 24	Michael Benson	Milford		On Mr Catherwood's order
1710	March 24	Elizabeth Gordon	Convoy		On Mr Catherwood's order
1712	March 24	Nancy Thompson	Convoy		On Mr Catherwood's order
	March 24	Andy Jack	Drumquin		£6-0s-0d for cabin
1691	March 24	James Mullen	Plumbridge		On Mr Catherwood's order
1720	March 24	Elizabeth O'Neill	L.Derry		On Mr Catherwood's order
	March 24	Jane O'Neill [scored out]	L.Derry		Jane O'Neill to go by the H. Thompson
	March 24	Daniel O'Neill	L.Derry	12	On Mr Catherwood's order
	March 24	James O'Neill	L.Derry	10	On Mr Catherwood's order
1724	March 24	Jane O'Neill	L.Derry	8	On Mr Catherwood's order
1713	March 24	Ann McNamee	NewtownStewart		On Mr Catherwood's order
1781	March 25	William Harkin	Donemana		£4-14s-0d
1782	March 25	Edward Hassard	Belleek		£4-15s-0d
1783	March 25	Mary McGrorty	Moville		£4-10s-0d
1784	March 25	Biddy McLaughlan	Malin	5	£4-0s-0d
1785	March 25	Fanny Nicholl	Stranorlar		£4-10s-0d
1786	March 25	James Creron	Ramelton		£4-15s-0d
1787	March 25	James Logue	Moville		£4-10s-0d

By the nineteenth century the emigrant trade in Derry depended to a large extent on people in North America paying the fare to bring out family and friends. Those passengers with 'On Mr Catherwood's order' against their name held pre-paid passage certificates purchased in the office of J & J Cooke's agent in Philadelphia, namely Andrew J. Catherwood of 62 North Second Street.

List of Passengers to sail from Londonderry Engaged at Philadelphia in December 1863 by Robert Taylor & Co.

Date (Engaged)	Name	Age	$	Ship	Date (to sail)	Address
20 November 1863	James Murray		27	Lady Emily Peel	28 June 1864	Derryhahan, Churchhill P.O., Co. Donegal
20 November 1863	Mary Murray		27	Lady Emily Peel	28 June 1864	Derryhahan, Churchhill P.O., Co. Donegal
7 December 1863	Susan Peoples		27	Minnehaha	1 April 1864	Killoughleck care Bernard Murray Letterkenny
8 December 1863	James Diver		27	Stadacona	30 March 1864	Patrick Boyce, Strabane
8 December 1863	Grace Diver		27	Stadacona	30 March 1864	Patrick Boyce, Strabane
8 December 1863	Mary Shields		27	Stadacona	30 March 1864	Carry Gart P.O., Co. Donegal
8 December 1863	Anthony Shields	10	18	Stadacona	30 March 1864	Carry Gart P.O., Co. Donegal
8 December 1863	Infant Shields	2 m	18	Stadacona	30 March 1864	Carry Gart P.O., Co. Donegal
8 December 1863	Grace Long	8	18	Stadacona	30 March 1864	care Jack Gallagher Dundoan, Carrygart
10 December 1863	Francis Shannon		27	Stadacona	30 March 1864	Pettigo, Co. Donegal
10 December 1863	Catharine Shannon		27	Stadacona	30 March 1864	Pettigo, Co. Donegal
15 December 1863	Stephen Green		27	Stadacona	30 March 1864	Aughadreena, Tamney P.O.
16 December 1863	Sarah McSorley		27	Stadacona	30 March 1864	Curr, Beragh P.O., Co. Tyrone
21 December 1863	Bernard McCollum		27	Stadacona	30 March 1864	Drumnasson, Creaslough P.O., Co. Donegal
21 December 1863	Anne McCollum		27	Stadacona	30 March 1864	Drumnasson, Creaslough P.O., Co. Donegal
21 December 1863	Dennis McCollum		27	Stadacona	30 March 1864	Drumnasson, Creaslough P.O., Co. Donegal
24 December 1863	Margaret Edminston		27	Stadacona	30 March 1864	Claudy near Strabane
26 December 1863	Mary A Cogan		27	Village Belle	9 August 1864	Carrigart P.O.
26 December 1863	James Cogan		27	Village Belle	9 August 1864	Carrigart P.O.
28 December 1863	Henry Slavin		27			for Patk Slavin, Kinnery, Drumore P.O., Co. Tyrone
30 December 1863	Sarah Coyle		27	Stadacona	30 March 1864	Drumditton, Carrigart P.O.
31 December 1863	Hugh McIntire		27	Stadacona	30 March 1864	Freast near Carrigart
31 December 1863	Mary McIntire		27	Stadacona	30 March 1864	Freast near Carrigart
31 December 1863	Catharine McIntire		27	Stadacona	30 March 1864	Freast near Carrigart
31 December 1863	Mary Freil		27	Stadacona	30 March 1864	Hugh Freil, Tunbane near Tamney, Co. Donegal
31 December 1863	James Freil		27	Stadacona	30 March 1864	Hugh Freil, Tunbane near Tamney, Co. Donegal
31 December 1863	Patrick Freil		27	Stadacona	30 March 1864	Hugh Freil, Tunbane near Tamney, Co. Donegal
31 December 1863	Catharine Freil		27	Stadacona	30 March 1864	Hugh Freil, Tunbane near Tamney, Co. Donegal
31 December 1863	Jane Carson		27	Stadacona	30 March 1864	care Capt Hasting, Letterkenny

The order book of Robert Taylor and Co. of Philadelphia, dating from November 1863 to April 1871, records the names and addresses of 5,184 Irish emigrants who were 'engaged' in Philadelphia, i.e. in receipt of pre-paid passage, to sail from Derry on ships of William McCorkell & Co.

The Derry to Glasgow passenger and livestock steamer was known as 'The Derry Boat' in Donegal and as 'The Scotch Boat' in Derry. It was an important part of Derry's maritime history; indeed for 137 years, running from 1829 until the autumn of 1966, there was a timetabled passenger service between Derry and Glasgow.

The Derry-Glasgow steerage passenger trade was initially dominated by the emigrant and the seasonal harvest worker, with the former travelling to Great Britain either to seek work or to board a liner for America. The seasonal harvest worker went over for a few months in the summer to work on farms in England or Scotland. From mid-August to mid-October these ships carried some 3,000 seasonal harvest labourers annually and, by 1850, the fare on the Derry-Glasgow route was one shilling and more than 8,000 passengers travelled yearly.

The cross-channel passenger trade from Derry was at its peak in 1910. At this time a passenger steamer left for England, from Derry, six times a week with sailings to Heysham, with Laird Line, every Monday and Thursday, to Fleetwood every Tuesday and Friday, and to Liverpool, with Belfast Steamship Company, every Wednesday and Saturday; and there were 6 passenger sailings each week to Greenock and Glasgow, with G & J Burns Ltd steamers departing every Monday and Thursday and Laird Line sailings every Tuesday, Wednesday, Friday and Saturday.

The decline in passenger services to England began in 1912 when the service to Fleetwood ended. Ten years later, in 1922, the steamers to Liverpool ceased carrying passengers but continued as cargo and livestock boats until 27 September 1965. The Heysham steamers stopped carrying passengers in the early 1930s but remained in operation for cargo until 11 October 1963.

Passenger sailings from Derry to Glasgow continued to thrive in the inter-war years. In 1922, the two old-established Glasgow companies, G & J Burns and Laird Line, who had pioneered passenger, goods and livestock routes between Scotland and Ireland amalgamated to form Burns and Laird Lines Ltd, and the Laird Line funnel of red, white and black was adopted by all of the ships of the fleet.

Scotch Boat Collision

On Saturday 16 September 1865, the *Garland*, a steamer belonging to the Derry and Glasgow Steam-packet Company, with a cargo of livestock and about 50 passengers, was heading down the Foyle from Derry quay bound for Glasgow. Between Quigley's Point and Whitecastle the *Garland* struck another steamer, the *Falcon* on the port bow, 'cutting her down almost to the water's edge.' The *Falcon*, owned by the City of Glasgow Steamship Company, was heading up the Foyle towards Derry 'crowded with Irish reapers returning from the Scotch harvest.' In total 17 men died in this incident; 2 were killed in the collision and a further 15 were drowned.

The *Derry Journal* of 20, 23, 27 and 30 September 1865 carried detailed reports of the incident, of the recovery of the bodies and of the inquests, including word-by-word reporting of witness statements.

The Gweedore Bar and Seasonal Migrants

James and Margaret Sweeney owned the Gweedore Bar in Waterloo Street, Derry from 1912 and they catered for seasonal migrants to Scotland from their home parish of Gweedore in northwest Donegal. James Sweeney also lent money to these migrants on their outward journey to Glasgow for fare, lodgings and drink, and on their return through Derry they would pay him back from wages earned in Scotland.

James Sweeney kept a record of this borrowing in the back of a large accounts ledger. These records begin in 1915 and end in 1945, and over this 30-year period James Sweeney recorded 1,555 entries in his ledger, *The Gweedore Book*. This book contains names of many islanders, off west coast of Donegal, from Gola, Owey, Inishsirrer, Cruit and Arranmore. Many left in the late autumn, winter, coinciding with end of the fishing season. In Arranmore there was a long tradition of 'tattie hoking,' and squads of men, women and children would leave every year for Scotland.

A Derry-Glasgow passenger service, by sea, continued until September 1966 when Burns and Laird transferred their last remaining passenger steamer on this route, the *Lairdsloch*, to the Dublin-Glasgow service.

Australia

The majority of 19th century Irish emigrants to Australia, New Zealand and South Africa departed from major British ports such as Glasgow, Liverpool, London, Plymouth and Southampton. Most emigrants from northwest Ireland destined for Australia, New Zealand or South Africa would have begun their journey on the cross-channel steamer out of Derry to either Glasgow or Liverpool.

However, in the period 1837 to 1845 the British Government fitted out ships to take selected emigrants from Irish ports such as Belfast, Cork, Derry and Limerick to New South Wales, Australia. Eligible emigrants and, in particular, "married agriculturists, not exceeding a certain age, with their wives and families" were given a free passage.

In 1837 and 1838 three ships provided by the government – *Adam Lodge*, *Parland* and *Susan* – sailed direct from Derry for New South Wales with, in total, nearly 1,000 emigrants. Emigrants sailing from Derry were selected, at the Custom House, by Dr James Hall, the government selection officer, with the selection process being "confined to a certain distance into the Counties of Derry, Tyrone and Donegal, it having been found inconvenient bringing people from remote parts."

For example, on 29 March 1837 the *Adam Lodge*, one of ten ships sent from British and Irish ports by the government to Australia in 1837, sailed from Derry. After a 107-day voyage she arrived at Port Jackson (i.e. Sydney Harbour) on 13 July 1837, with 405 passengers, consisting of 197 adults and 208 children under 14 years. During the passage, there were 30 deaths on board: 25 children, 4 women and 1 man, namely John Park of Derry.

A report in the *Londonderry Sentinel* of 15 July 1848 confirms that during the famine years children were sent from the workhouse in Derry to Australia:

'Londonderry' from an original sketch by John Nixon

This image of Derry dates back to just before the construction of its first bridge in 1790. The ferry boat, carrying two horses and five passengers, is making its way across the River Foyle, and the elegant spire of St Columb's Cathedral dominates the skyline. The larger ship in the foreground could well be destined for America.

***Minnehaha*, the flagship of William McCorkell & Company, grain and emigration merchants, Londonderry**
Courtesy of John McCorkell, www.mccorkellline.com

The McCorkell family commissioned oil paintings of many, but not all, ships which sailed under the McCorkell flag from 1834 to 1897. Marine artist, Joseph Joshua Sempill (buried in Derry City Cemetery) painted the *Minnehaha* in its full glory as a passenger carrying clipper, with three sets of full sails.

Anchor Line advertising poster depicting *Caledonia*

The Anchor Line, twin-screw steamship *Caledonia*, 9,223 tons, 500 feet in length, made 115 passenger sailings from Glasgow, via Moville (Londonderry), to New York from 1905 to 1914. In August 1914 the *Caledonia* was requisitioned as a troopship, and on 4 December 1916 she was torpedoed and sunk off Malta.

Scotch Boat *Lairdsbank* at Derry quay in summer 1963
Courtesy of Samuel P. Mitchell

The Scotch Boat was an important part of Derry's maritime history; indeed for 137 years, running from 1829 until the autumn of 1966, there was a timetabled passenger service between Derry and Glasgow.

"EMIGRANTS FROM THE LONDONDERRY WORKHOUSE TO AUSTRALIA –
On Tuesday, 27 young girls, accompanied by an elderly female, from the Londonderry Workhouse, embarked in the steamer *John Munn*, via Liverpool, to Dublin, from whence they will proceed to Plymouth, and sail for Australia, under the government grant of emigration. Their appearance does much credit to Miss McCandless, the matron, under whose superintendence their outfit was prepared, and who has won for herself "golden opinions" by her kindness and affability."

George Fletcher Moore

The journey of the well-to-do could be quite leisurely. George Fletcher Moore, born at Bond's Glen near Claudy, County Londonderry in 1798, set sail from Dublin for Western Australia in June 1830 with four servants and his dog. The Swan River Colony had just been established with a settlement at Perth in 1829. He soon established a routine on his 85-day voyage: rising at 6am; breakfast at 8am; then he wrote and studied in his cabin; dined with the captain and first mate at 3pm; tea by candlelight at 7pm; then he went on deck to chat or to do gymnastics on the ropes.

He purchased animals at the Cape (South Africa) to stock his farm. He arrived in Western Australia in good heart. "My cheeks" he said "have plumped out and I have no longer the sallow visage of the student but the ruddy hue of the farmer." Moore flourished in his new environment. By 1836 he was the largest flock holder in the Swan River with 800 sheep. In 1832 he was appointed civil commissioner and played an important conciliatory role in negotiating treaties between the Aborigines and settlers of Western Australia. In 1846 a disgruntled Scot complained to the Colonial Office that Western Australia had a complete Irish Protestant government.

Emigration in the Age of Steam: In the late-19th and early-20th Century

From 1861 right through to 1939 ocean-going liners called at Moville, in the deeper waters of Lough Foyle, some 18 miles downstream from Derry, to pick up emigrants who were ferried from Derry in paddle tenders. During this period, at various times, four shipping lines – Anchor Line, Anchor-Donaldson Line, Allan Line and Dominion Line – made Derry a stage on the voyage from Liverpool or Glasgow to Canada or the United States.

From the 1860s the growth of traffic through Derry port was increasingly dependent upon the transatlantic steamers calling at Moville to pick up passengers and mails on their way to Canada and USA. There was a steady growth in tonnage of transatlantic steamers calling at Moville, rising from 200,000 tons in 1866 to a peak of 940,000 tons in 1905. Although the tonnage of transatlantic liners calling at Moville never surpassed this figure again, it did remain at a consistently high level (apart from during the First World War years of 1915 to 1918 when all emigration ceased) of over 600,000 tons per annum until 1931, when there was a dramatic fall off in transatlantic liners calling at Lough Foyle. Indeed, in 1925, the tonnage of liners calling at Moville peaked at 825,000 tons, a figure that was only ever exceeded in the years between 1902 and 1906 inclusive. In 1931, however, legislation ending uncontrolled immigration to the US became fully operational.

By making Derry a 'port of call,' where steamers took but a few hours to embark and disembark passengers at Moville, on voyages from Liverpool and Glasgow to North

Anchor Line poster

ANCHOR LINE OF ROYAL MAIL STEAMERS.

MONTREAL OCEAN STEAM SHIP COMPANY.

"ALLAN" ROYAL MAIL LINE.

SHIP.	TONS.
SARDINIAN	4500
CIRCASSIAN	4000
CANADIAN	3000
POLYNESIAN	4500
SARMATIAN	4300
CASPIAN	3500
SCANDINAVIAN	3500
PRUSSIAN	3500
AUSTRIAN	3000
NESTORIAN	3000

SHIP.	TONS.
PERUVIAN	4000
MORAVIAN	4000
HIBERNIAN	3500
NOVA SCOTIAN	3500
NEWFOUNDLAND	1500
CORINTHIAN	2800
MANITOBAN	3000
PHŒNICIAN	2800
WALDENSIAN	3000
ACADIAN	2800

SHORTEST OCEAN PASSAGE TO CANADA AND THE UNITED STATES.

LIVERPOOL, QUEBEC, AND PORTLAND.

Summer Arrangements. (From April to November.)

From LIVERPOOL every THURSDAY. | From QUEBEC every SATURDAY.

Winter Arrangements. (From November to April.)

From LIVERPOOL every THURSDAY. | From PORTLAND (U.S.), every SATURDAY.

LIVERPOOL, HALIFAX (N.S.), AND BALTIMORE.

This route affords a *most convenient means of communication* with the SOUTHERN STATES of AMERICA.

From LIVERPOOL every alternate TUESDAY. | From BALTIMORE every alternate TUESDAY.

CABIN FARES.

According to position of Sleeping Cabins and number of Berths in same, all having full privileges in Saloon. Children under Twelve years, Half-fare; Infants under Two years, Free.

Quebec (direct)	£12 0 0	£15 0 0	£18 0 0	St. John's, N.F. (direct)	£13 0 0	15 0 0
Halifax (direct)	12 0 0	15 0 0	18 0 0	Baltimore, via Halifax	£12 0 0	15 0 0 . 18 0 0
Portland (direct)	12 0 0	15 0 0	18 0 0			

THROUGH TICKETS (Single Journey), including 1st Class Rail.

Portland, via Quebec	£13 18 0	£16 8 0	£19 8 0	Collingwood, Canada	£14 10 6	£17 0 0	£20 0 0
Montreal	12 14 6	15 4 6	18 14 6	*Detroit, Michigan	14 17 6	17 0 0	20 0 0
*Boston	12 12 0	15 10 0	18 10 0	*Chicago, Illinois	15 15 0	17 10 0	20 0 0
*New York	12 12 0	15 10 0	18 10 0	*St. Louis, Missouri	17 0 0	18 10 0	20 10 0
*Philadelphia	12 0 0	15 0 0	18 18 0	*St. Paul, Minnesota	18 0 0	19 10 0	21 10 0
Kingston, Canada	13 16 0	16 10 0	19 10 0	*Milwaukee, Wis.	16 0 0	18 0 0	20 0 0
Ottawa	13 13 0	16 10 0	19 10 0	*Omaha, Nebraska	18 10 0	20 0 0	21 10 0
Toronto	13 0 0	16 10 0	19 10 0	*San Francisco, Cal.	36 10 0	38 10 0	41 0 0
London	14 0 0	16 10 0	19 10 0	Victoria, Brit. Col.	41 10 0	43 10 0	45 10 0
Hamilton	14 0 0	16 10 0	19 10 0	St. John, N.B. via Halifax	13 0 0	16 0 0	19 0 0
Sarnia, Canada	14 17 6	17 0 0	20 0 0	St. John, N.B. via Rimouski	14 0 0	17 0 0	20 0 0

And to all Stations in Canada and the States.

*PASSENGERS FOR THESE DESTINATIONS HAVE THE OPTION OF ROUTE EITHER VIA QUEBEC OR BALTIMORE.

TWENTY CUBIC FEET OF LUGGAGE ALLOWED EACH PASSENGER, ANY EXCESS CHARGED AT THE RATE OF ONE SHILLING PER FOOT.

Berths can be secured only upon payment of a deposit of £5 each Berth, and holders of Return Tickets can be Booked only upon their exchanging those for Passage Tickets.

OCEAN RETURN TICKETS issued at £22, £25, or £30, available for Twelve Months, from any of the American or Canadian Ports from which the Company's Steamers sail.

☞ *Passengers taking "RETURN TICKETS" by this line of Steamers can go out by way of Quebec, and return by way of Baltimore, or Halifax, or vice versâ.*

Passengers booked through to all parts of Canada and the United States, China, Japan, and Australia at lowest rates.

For Information apply to

ALLANS, RAE, & CO.	QUEBEC.	H. & A. ALLAN	MONTREAL.	S. CUNARD & CO.	HALIFAX.
H. & A. ALLAN	PORTLAND.	ALLAN & CO.	CHICAGO.	A. SCHUMACHER & CO.	BALTIMORE.
		AMBROSE SHEA	ST. JOHN'S, N.F.	WM. THOMSON & CO.	ST. JOHN, N.B.
GUSTAVE BOSSANGE, 16, Rue 4 Septembre	PARIS.	JAMES SCOTT & CO.			QUEENSTOWN.
MONTGOMERIE & GREENHORNE,		J. & A. ALLAN, 70, Great Clyde Street			GLASGOW.
17, Gracechurch Street	LONDON.	ALLAN BROTHERS & CO., 50, Foyle Street, LONDONDERRY.			

ALLAN BROTHERS & CO., ALEXANDRA BUILDINGS, JAMES STREET, LIVERPOOL.

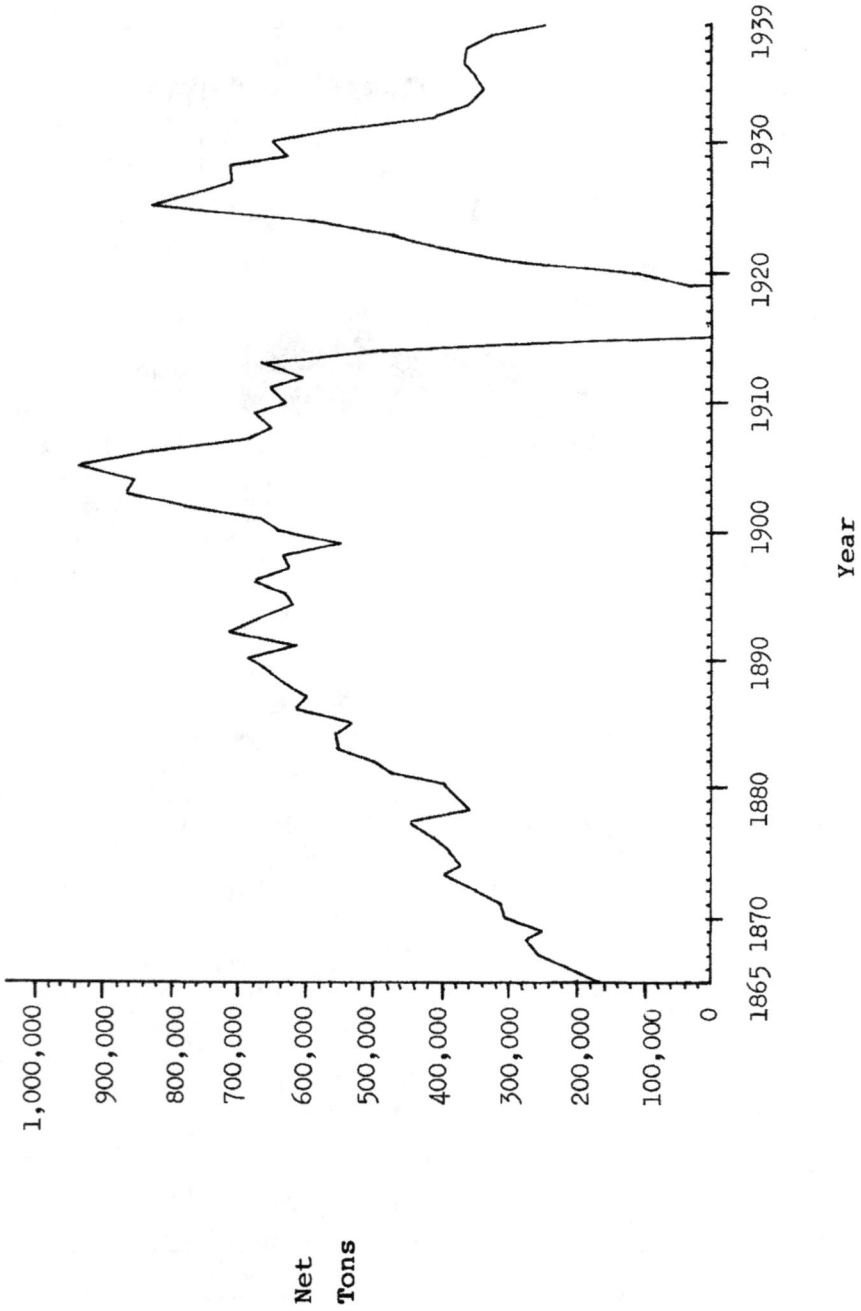

Tonnage of Transatlantic Passenger Steamers Calling at the Port of Londonderry 1865 to 1939

America, a sustainable business grew which linked Derry to Britain and to northern Europe. As early as 1868 the Anchor Line offered a "transmigrant" service from Scandinavian ports, bringing passengers from Oslo and Gothenburg to Leith and then transferring them by rail to Glasgow. Allan Line ships carried many German, Scandinavian and Russian emigrants who had travelled to Liverpool by rail from the east coast port of Hull.

Much of the emigrant business that had drifted away to Liverpool was now brought back to Derry. In 1883, emigrant departures from Derry exceeded the number that went through the port in the peak famine year of 1847 (12,385); when 15,217 emigrants boarded 154 steamers calling at Moville, with 10,496 destined for the United States and 4,721 for Canada.

The Importance of Derry's Railways

The railway had a vital role to play in the development of transatlantic passenger services as the railway was the usual form of transport by which emigrants reached Derry.

The rail network that converged on Derry, by 1910, was the product of a number of small companies who, on a piecemeal basis, built up a railway system that confirmed and reinforced Derry's position as the hub of northwest Ireland and as a departure point for emigrants to North America.

The Great Northern Railway Company connected Derry, via Strabane and Omagh, to both Belfast and Dublin from its terminus on Foyle Road. The Midland Railway (Northern Counties Committee) ran the railway service from Derry, via Coleraine, to Belfast from its station in the Waterside, and operated the Strabane to Derry section of the former Donegal Railway (on the east bank of the Foyle) from its station at Victoria Road. The County Donegal Railways Joint Committee (from 1906) then ran trains from Strabane westward to Glenties, Killybegs and Ballyshannon. The Londonderry and Lough Swilly Railway Company connected Derry, from its Strand Road station, to Buncrana with extensions to Letterkenny (in 1883), Carndonagh (in 1901) and Burtonport (in 1904).

This extensive rail network carried intending emigrants, from the northern half of Ireland, towards Derry. Hence, the passenger manifests of transatlantic liners departing Derry, listed, not only passengers from the city's traditional catchment areas of Counties Derry, Donegal and Tyrone, but also emigrants from the other six counties of Ulster (Antrim, Armagh, Cavan, Down, Fermanagh and Monaghan), the cities of Belfast and Dublin, the northern counties of Connacht such as Leitrim and Sligo and the northern counties of Leinster such as Longford and Meath.

Derry now became the major emigration port for the northern half of Ireland. By 1900, the Steamship Companies and Railway Companies in Ireland were offering cheap rail tickets to those intending emigrants, embarking at Derry, who boarded trains at railway stations north of a line which stretched from Sligo on the west coast to Dublin on the east coast. In effect, it was assumed that if you lived north of this line you emigrated from Derry, and if you lived in the southern half of Ireland you embarked at Queenstown (now Cobh).

Annual Emigration Reports from the Port of Londonderry published in the *Londonderry Sentinel* show that between 1877 and 1897 inclusive 193,887 passengers embarked at Moville for North America; with 153,886 destined for USA and 40,001 to Canada.

The Rail Network from Derry in 1910

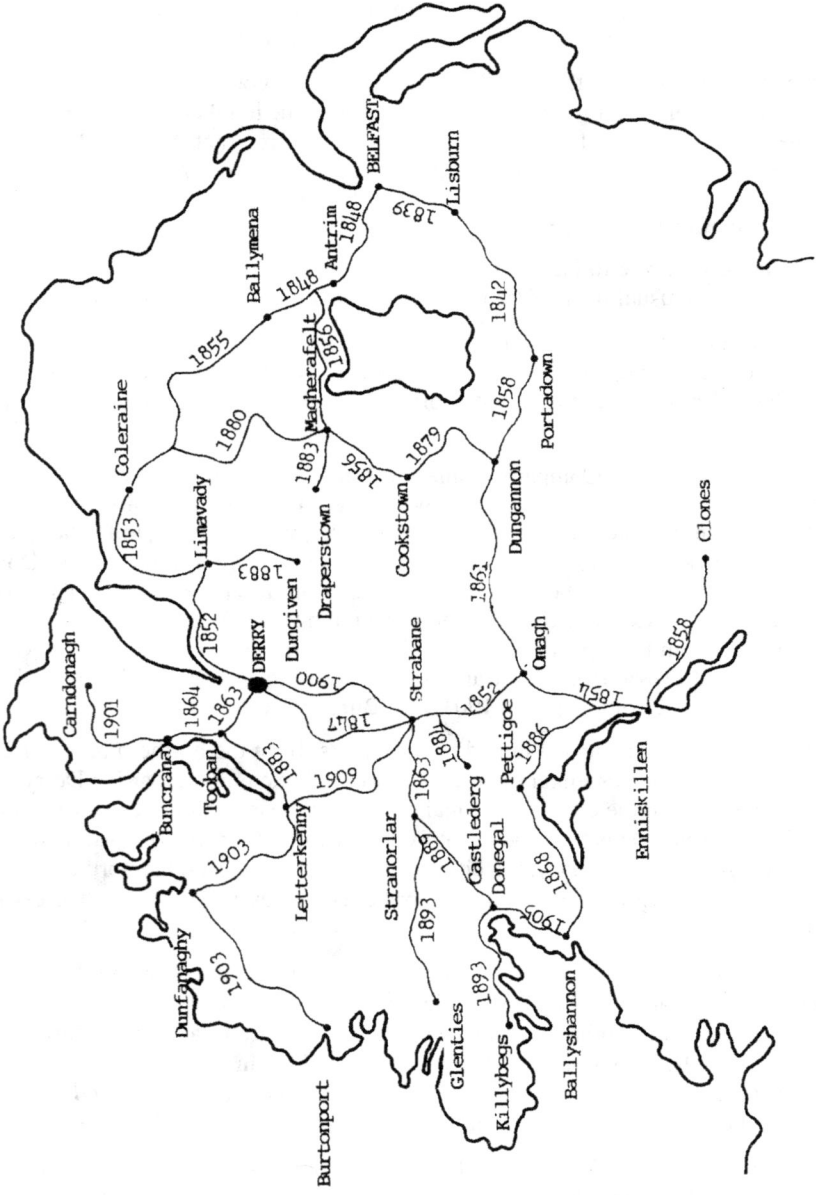

BELFAST
Lisburn 1839
Antrim 1848
Ballymena 1848
Magherafelt 1856
Coleraine 1855
1853
Limavady 1880
1883
Draperstown 1856
Cookstown 1879
Portadown 1842
1858
Dungannon 1861
Omagh 1854
Clones 1858
Enniskillen
Pettigoe 1886
Donegal 1889
Castlederg 1884
Strabane 1852
DERRY 1847
Dungiven 1883
1852
1863 1864
1900
1901
Carndonagh
Buncrana
Tooban
1883
Letterkenny 1909
Stranorlar
1889
1863
1893
Glenties
Killybegs 1893
Ballyshannon 1905
Donegal 1889
1868
1903
Dunfanaghy
Burtonport 1903

KEY
• Town with rail link
1847 Date of completion of rail link

24

Government statistics further record that from 1851 to 1920, 407,781 people from northwest Ireland (i.e. Counties Derry, Donegal and Tyrone) emigrated to lands beyond the British Isles.

For many emigrants the boarding houses in Bridge Street, was where they slept on their arrival, usually by train, in Derry. At the bottom of Bridge Street was the jetty, at the 'Transatlantic Tenders' shed (built 1904 and destroyed by fire in 1961) on Abercorn Quay, beside the Great Northern Railway station, where the tenders of the Moville Steamship Company and, from 1928, of the Anchor Line took emigrants to Moville to board the liners that left weekly for the USA and Canada.

The Shipping Lines

In September 1854, the Allan Line, or the Montreal Ocean Steamship Company, introduced weekly steamship sailings from Liverpool, calling at Moville from 1861, to Quebec and Montreal during the summer and to Halifax, Nova Scotia and Portland, Maine during the winter.

In *Derry Almanac and Directory* of 1861 the Montreal Ocean Steamship Company was advertising "All the Year Round, Every Friday from Londonderry to America" the "Cheapest and Shortest Sea Passage by Steam." By 1890, the Allan Line advertised that the average passage time from 'Londonderry to Canada Direct Every Friday' was seven days, and the fare charged was £4 10 shillings 'Steerage,' £7 7 shillings 'Second Cabin' and 10 to 18 Guineas 'Saloon.'

Direct departures from Derry on Allan Line ships ended with the First World War. In 1917, the Allan Line merged with the Canadian Pacific Line. By 1920, Canadian Pacific Line, retaining Allan Line office at 50 Foyle Street, Derry were advertising 'through bookings from Ireland to Canada,' and, by 1923, they had vacated their Derry Office and were advertising sailings from 'Belfast to Canada fortnightly during season.'

The Glasgow shipping company of Handysides & Henderson, in 1856, inaugurated a new mail, cargo and passenger service, the "Anchor Line of Steam Packets" between Glasgow and New York. From 1866, the company's Glasgow to New York steamships started calling at Moville and continued to do so until 1939.

Off Moville, prior to the First World War, Anchor Line ships, with their all black funnels, could be distinguished from the Allan Line ships with their distinctive funnels of red with narrow white band below a black top.

In 1916 the Anchor Line and another Glasgow company, the Donaldson Line, merged their services to Canada and formed a joint company, Anchor-Donaldson, to operate the route. Four Donaldson ships, the *Letitia*, *Saturnia*, *Cassandra* and *Athenia*, were transferred to the new shipping line.

By 1930, the Anchor Line were promoting their 'Londonderry & Belfast to New York' service on their 'New Oil-Burning Liners "California," "Caledonia," "Cameronia," "Tuscania," "Transylvania," – all 16,700 Tons;' and the Anchor-Donaldson Line their 'Londonderry and Belfast to Canada' service which sailed 'in Summer to Quebec and Montreal; in Winter to Halifax and St. John, N.B., or Portland, Maine.'

List of Passengers who departed Londonderry on 5 April 1930 for Halifax and New York on Anchor Line ship *Tuscania*

Name	Address	Age	Profession	Destination Port
Hugh Kelly	Balnamore, Ballymoney	33	Motorman	New York
James Kearney	Glar, Donegal	31	Farm Labourer	New York
George Morrow	Lough Eske, Co. Donegal	26	Farm Labourer	New York
Michael Smith	Killnebber, Cavan	33	Contractor	New York
Annie Smith	Killnebber, Cavan	27	Housewife	New York
Francis Smith	Killnebber, Cavan	1		New York
Mary Smith	Killnebber, Cavan	6 wks		New York
Ellen McElnay	Bushmills, Co. Antrim	26	Domestic	New York
David Sharpe	31 Caulfield Terrace, Newry	29	Constable	Halifax
Annie Sharpe	31 Caulfield Terrace, Newry	26	Housewife	Halifax
Robert Hasson	Park, Co. Derry	26	Farm Labourer	Halifax
John Hamilton	Omagh, Co. Tyrone	22	Farm Labourer	Halifax
William Steele	Gortin, Co. Tyrone	19	Farm Labourer	Halifax
Alexander Taylor	Quigley's Point, Co Donegal	19	Labourer	Halifax
Daniel Scanlon	Ballybofey, Co. Donegal	25	Farm Labourer	Halifax
Charles Meehan	Letterbarrow, Co. Donegal	23	Farm Labourer	Halifax
Allan McKeown	Abbey St, Clones, Monaghan	23	Painter	Halifax
Thomas Blair	Macosquin, Coleraine	20	Shop Assistant	Halifax
John Taylor	Aghadowey, Co. Derry	36	Farm Labourer	Halifax
Thomas Campbell	Ringsend, Garvagh	40	Farmer	Halifax
Agnes Campbell	Ringsend, Garvagh	30	Housewife	Halifax
Henry Blair	Portrush, Co. Antrim	24	Farm Labourer	Halifax
Jennie Blair	Portrush, Co. Antrim	23	Housewife	Halifax
Sarah Buchanan	Captain Street, Coleraine	17	Book-keeper	Halifax
Catherine Buchanan	Captain Street, Coleraine	18	Shop Assistant	Halifax
Mary McLoughlin	Co. Donegal	20	Domestic	Halifax
William McClean	Claudy, Co. Derry	16	Farm Labourer	Halifax
John Patrick	Seskinore, Omagh, Tyrone	20	Farm Labourer	Halifax
Robert Ross	Lisnagrot, Kilrea, Co. Derry	24	Farm Labourer	Halifax
James Ross	Lisnagrot, Kilrea, Co. Derry	21	Farm Labourer	Halifax
Bernard Donaghey	Patrick Street, Strabane	27	Butcher	Halifax
William O'Neill	Butcher Street, Strabane	26	Labourer	Halifax
James O'Neill	Butcher Street, Strabane	27	Labourer	Halifax
Robert Smith	Garvagh, Co. Derry	21	Farm Labourer	Halifax
James McManus	Letterbarrow, Co. Donegal	25	Farm Labourer	Halifax
Mary Ward	Donegal, Co. Donegal	19	Domestic	Halifax
Patrick Meehan	Letterbarrow, Co. Donegal	20	Farm Labourer	Halifax
William Scott	Laghey, Co. Donegal	33	Farm Labourer	Halifax
Essie Harron	Laghey, Co. Donegal	25	Domestic	Halifax
Maggie Burns	Mountcharles, Co. Donegal	27	Domestic	Halifax
Neil Gallagher	Letterbarrow, Co. Donegal	23	Farm Labourer	Halifax
Alex Stevenson	Dromore, Co. Tyrone	23	Farm Labourer	Halifax
Elizabeth Kennedy	Trenta, Letterkenny, Donegal	25	Domestic	Halifax
Ellen McDaid	Glengad, Culkeeny, Donegal	30	Domestic	Halifax
Bridget Bannon	Ballyconnell, Co. Cavan	18	Domestic	Halifax
Owen Carrigan	Dowra, Co. Cavan	26	Farm Labourer	Halifax
Bessie McHugh	Dowra, Co. Cavan	31	Domestic	Halifax
Henry Patton	33 Aberfoyle Tce, L'Derry	18	Labourer	Halifax

Manifests listing passengers who departed Derry, at Moville, for USA and Canada between 1890 and 1939 are held in the records of the Board of Trade. These lists, from 1922, record the address in Ireland of all embarking passengers; prior to this the only clue to family origin was either 'Nationality' or 'Country of Last Permanent Residence'.

From 1887, departing from Derry every alternate Friday, the Dominion Line of Liverpool was operating a passenger service to Canada (to Quebec and Montreal during the summer and to Halifax and Portland during the winter). By 1902, however, the Dominion Line was absorbed into the White Star Line and its transatlantic ships picked up passengers at Cobh, not Derry.

White Star Line and Cunard Line

The main competitors of the Anchor Line and Allan Line for Irish passenger traffic, at turn of 20th century, were the Cunard Line and White Star Line. These companies operated out of Liverpool and their ships called at Queenstown (Cobh) on their way to the USA and Canada.

An examination of shipping advertisements placed in *Derry Journal* and *Londonderry Sentinel* of November 1910 demonstrates this: The White Star Line in advertising its Liverpool, via Queenstown, to New York and Boston service boasted, 'OLYMPIC 45,000 TONS & TITANIC 45,000 TONS – Largest Steamers in the World Building;' and the Cunard Line proclaimed, 'LUSITANIA' & 'MAURETANIA' are the largest and fastest vessels in the world from Liverpool via Queenstown to New York and Boston.'

Titanic

In 1912, one million people emigrated, in 1,280 ships, from Europe to North America, with 30,000 of this total departing Ireland, of whom 14,590 embarked at Cobh, 5,895 at Derry and 5,767 at Belfast.

On 11April 1912, 113 Irish emigrants, mainly from the west and south of Ireland, boarded the ill-fated RMS *Titanic* at Queenstown (Cobh), of whom 40 survived. Only two of the Irish passengers – one from County Donegal, with a Derry city connection, and the other from County Down – were from Ulster; emigrants from Ulster in this period were served by ships calling at Derry and Belfast.

Among those to lose their life in the sinking of the ship was Donegal-born Neal McNamee who had worked in the Derry branch, at 5 Bishop Street, of world-famous tea company, Liptons. Neal boarded the *Titanic* in Southampton; he was moving to New York with his new wife Eileen (formerly O'Leary) to work for Liptons.

Tourism

From the early 1900s, the links forged by mass emigration together with Derry's position as an Irish transatlantic hub became a tourist asset. The shipping companies printed posters emphasising the style and romance of the ocean liners to encourage holidays abroad. One such poster campaign proclaimed: "Come Back to Erin: ANCHOR LINE New York and Londonderry".

The outbreak of war in 1939 meant the end of this emigrant and tourist trade. With the return of peace, in 1945, the transatlantic liners didn't come back to Derry. In the 1950s and early 1960s emigrants from all over Ireland headed, by train, to Cobh.

Anchor Line tender *Seamore* berthed at 'Transatlantic Tenders' shed at Abercorn Quay

Courtesy of Bigger and McDonald collection, Derry Central Library, LibrariesNI

In May 1928 the Anchor Line acquired the Clyde Shipping Company's paddle steamer *America*. It renamed her *Seamore* and stationed her at Abercorn Quay, adjoining the Great Northern Railway Station, to ferry passengers and emigrants between Derry and Moville. She was a typical tug-tender with one funnel and a small saloon for passengers on her after deck.

Anchor Line tender *Seamore*, filled to capacity, heads down the Foyle towards Moville

Courtesy of Bigger and McDonald collection, Derry Central Library, LibrariesNI

From 1928 to 1939 the Anchor Line's tender *Seamore* carried emigrants from Derry to Moville to connect with either Anchor Line ships destined for the United States or Anchor-Donaldson Line ships for Canada.

The Monteith family, destined for Halifax, Canada, aboard the Anchor Line tender *Seamore*
Courtesy of Bigger and McDonald collection, Derry Central Library, LibrariesNI

This photograph with caption "The Monteith family, from Castlederg, who sailed from Moville on Saturday on the Anchor Donaldson liner for Canada" was published in *Derry Standard* of 15 April 1929

Grieving emigrants departing Derry aboard the Anchor Line tender *Seamore*
Courtesy of Bigger and McDonald collection, Derry Central Library, LibrariesNI

This photograph with caption "Some passengers were overcome with grief as the tender moved off from Derry Quay" was published in *Derry Standard* of 12 September 1938

www.ingramcontent.com/pod-product-compliance
Lightning Source LLC
Chambersburg PA
CBHW060813280326
41934CB00010B/2676